www.ingramcontent.com/pod-product-compliance
Lightning Source LLC
Chambersburg PA
CBHW061943280526
45787CB00004B/1702
* 9 7 8 1 5 3 3 6 3 2 9 5 1 *